Poundmaker

Terry Barber

MAPLE LEAF SERIES

Poundmaker is published by
Grass Roots Press, a division of Literacy Services of Canada Ltd.

PHONE 1–888–303–3213
WEBSITE www.grassrootsbooks.net

ACKNOWLEDGMENTS

We acknowledge the financial support of the Government of Canada through the Canada Book Fund (CBF) for our publishing activities.

Produced with the assistance of
the Government of Alberta, Alberta
Multimedia Development Fund.

**Government
of Alberta** ■

Editor: Dr. Pat Campbell
Image research: Dr. Pat Campbell
Book design: Lara Minja

Library and Archives Canada Cataloguing in Publication

Barber, Terry, date
    Poundmaker / Terry Barber.

(Maple leaf series)
ISBN 978–1–926583–40–2

    1. Poundmaker, Cree Chief, 1826–1886. 2. Cree Indians—Kings and rulers—Biography. 3. Cree Indians—Prairie Provinces—Biography. 4. Readers for new literates. I. Title. II. Series: Barber, Terry, 1950– . Maple Leaf series.

PE1126.N43B36625 2011   428.6'2   C2011–904441–2

Printed in Canada

Contents

Early Years...5

Poundmaker and Crowfoot.................................13

A Time of Change 21

Treaty 6.................................23

Chief Poundmaker 31

The Northwest Rebellion of 1885 35

Broken Promises, Broken Spirit 41

Cree men trap bison.

Early Years

The medicine man lives with the Cree
people. He prays for bison to return.
When the bison return, he helps to
trap them in a **pound**. In 1842, the
medicine man and his wife have a son.
They call their son Poundmaker.

CANADA

Woodland Cree

Plains Cree

Cree bands cover much of the Prairies.

Early Years

Poundmaker's parents die when he is young. A Plains Cree band takes care of Poundmaker. The Cree live in bands or hunting groups for most of the year. Poundmaker helps to provide food for his band. Like his father, he learns to hunt bison.

The Plains Cree lived in the West.

Cree men hunt with guns, and bows and arrows.

Early Years

The Cree depend on the bison.
Hunters ride toward a herd of
bison. The bison run. Dust fills the
air. Hunters fire their guns. Bison
fall. After a hunt, there is a feast.
Poundmaker is one of the best hunters
in his band.

The Cree
also make
clothes, rope, and
tools from the
bison.

The warriors return to their camp after a raid.

Early Years

Poundmaker is also a warrior.
The Blackfoot and Cree are enemies.
The two tribes **raid** each other's
camps. They steal horses. They steal
women and children. Many warriors
die. These raids go on and on.

Crowfoot

Poundmaker and Crowfoot

The year is 1873. Poundmaker is
30 years old. The Plains Cree and
the Blackfoot begin peace talks.
The Blackfoot Chief is called
Crowfoot. His son is killed in a battle.
Crowfoot meets Poundmaker.
Crowfoot thinks Poundmaker looks
like his lost son.

A Blackfoot camp.

Poundmaker and Crowfoot

Crowfoot can see that Poundmaker is a leader. Poundmaker is a good speaker. He is a good storyteller. And he is a good drummer. He shares food and goods with others. Crowfoot invites Poundmaker to live at his camp for a winter.

A Blackfoot warrior.

Poundmaker and Crowfoot

Poundmaker's life changes. Crowfoot adopts Poundmaker as his son. Some Blackfoot warriors are angry. They want to kill Poundmaker. But they come to accept Poundmaker. They see Poundmaker is a good man.

Poundmaker learns the Blackfoot language.

Poundmaker and one of his wives.

Poundmaker and Crowfoot

After the winter, Poundmaker returns
to his own people. He returns with
gifts from Crowfoot. He returns with
a message of peace. Poundmaker says
that Crowfoot wants to end the raids.
In time, the Blackfoot and Cree accept
each other.

Poundmaker
has two wives.

Settlers in Winnipeg, Manitoba.
1872

A Time of Change

Peace comes in a time of great change. More white settlers arrive. They kill the bison and sell the hides. The bison herds grow smaller. A way of life passes. The Cree must find a new way to live.

By the 1880s, the bison are almost gone.

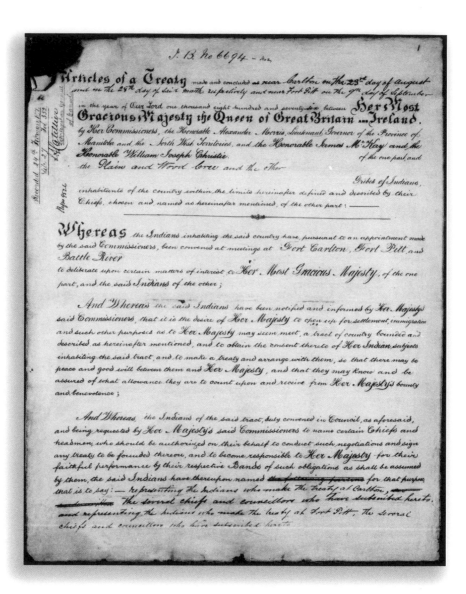

The first page of Treaty 6.

Treaty 6

The Government of Canada wants
the Cree to give up their land. The
government wants more land for
white settlers. The Cree Chiefs meet
with the government. The government
wants the Cree to sign a **treaty**.
This treaty is called Treaty 6.

Poundmaker

24

Treaty 6

The government wants the Cree to live on **reserves**. Poundmaker **protests**: "This is our land! It isn't a piece of **pemmican** to be cut off and given in little pieces back to us. It is ours and we will take what we want."

Treaty 6 promises 640 acres of reserve land for each Cree family.

Cree people learn to farm.

Treaty 6

Poundmaker demands support in return for land. He wants a good treaty for his people. The government wants to start a farming program. The government promises to teach the Cree people how to farm. The government promises farm supplies.

The government promises free medicine.

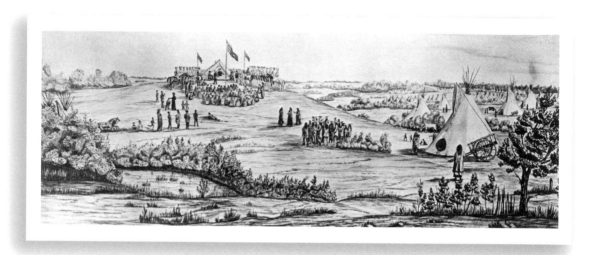

Cree Chiefs sign Treaty 6.

Treaty 6

In 1876, Poundmaker and the other Cree Chiefs sign Treaty 6. Before they sign, Poundmaker asks for one last promise. He wants the government to provide food in times of hunger. The government adds this promise to the treaty.

The government passes the **Indian** Act in 1876.

Poundmaker talks to his men on the reserve.

Chief Poundmaker

In 1879, Poundmaker and his people
move to a reserve. They farm the
land. The soil is poor. The crops
are poor. Many people go hungry.
The government provides little food.
The government breaks its promise.

By 1880,
Poundmaker
is a chief.

Chiefs Big Bear and Poundmaker.

Chief Poundmaker

Poundmaker knows there is strength in numbers. In 1884, he unites with Chief Big Bear and other leaders. The government must listen to a united people. But it does not listen. The government does little to help the Cree people.

Poundmaker becomes active in Indian politics.

Louis Riel
1884

The Northwest Rebellion of 1885

In 1884, a **Métis** leader sends a list of demands to the government. His name is Louis Riel. The Métis want what the Indians want. Canada does not meet the demands. Some of the Métis leaders decide to use force.

The Cree talk about their demands at a thirst dance.

The Métis win the battle at Duck Lake.

The Northwest Rebellion of 1885

The Métis want Poundmaker to lead his men into war. Poundmaker does not want his people to suffer. Some Cree join the Métis in battle. Most do not. The first battle is at Duck Lake. Poundmaker does not lift a weapon.

The Duck Lake battle is on March 27, 1885.

Poundmaker gives himself up.

The Northwest Rebellion of 1885

The last battle is in May 1885. Poundmaker gives himself up. He is put on trial. He says: "I am not guilty. You did not catch me. I gave myself up. You have got me because I wanted peace."

The last battle is at Batoche.

Poundmaker in prison.
1885

Broken Promises, Broken Spirit

Poundmaker is found guilty of **treason**. Poundmaker must serve three years in prison. He becomes sick. His spirit is broken. He is let out of prison after one year.

Poundmaker will not let the prison guards cut his hair.

Two Cree men.
1884

Broken Promises, Broken Spirit

In 1886, Poundmaker is out of jail. Poundmaker's world has changed. The Indian way of life is gone. His peoples' spirit is broken. No hope fills their eyes. They cannot live on promises.

Poundmaker's grave.

Broken Promises, Broken Spirit

Poundmaker visits Crowfoot. The Blackfoot Chief is broken, too. Poundmaker dies on July 4, 1886 in Crowfoot's camp. Poundmaker is just 44 years old. The Plains Cree lose a great leader. Poundmaker finally finds peace.

Glossary

Indian: Indigenous People in Canada who are not Inuit or Métis. The term First Nations has replaced the word Indian.

Métis: In the 1800s, Métis means a person of mixed Indian and European ancestry.

pemmican: dried meat, berries, and fat mixed together.

pound: a space used to trap and kill bison.

protest: to complain about something.

raid: to attack suddenly.

rebellion: an open fight against one's government.

reserve: land set aside by treaty for First Nations people.

treason: betrayal of one's country.

treaty: an agreement between two or more nations.

Talking About the Book

What did you learn about Poundmaker?

What challenges did Poundmaker face in his life?

Describe how the life of the Cree people changed after the settlers arrived.

What did you learn about Treaty 6?

How do you think Poundmaker felt about signing Treaty 6?

What did Treaty 6 promise the Cree people? Were these promises kept?

Do you think Poundmaker was a peacemaker or a warrior?

Picture Credits